Praise for
What Happens in Tomorrow World?

"A fun to read, delightful, and most definitely wisdom-filled story! Once I began . . . just couldn't put it down. So many wonderful life lessons, including mentorship that might just be some of the most profound I've ever read. Pay particular attention to Sage, as well as a nine-year-old Catch, and in one quick reading you'll encounter the ingredients for living a successful, happy life. Fantastic!"

—Bob Burg, coauthor of the Go-Giver series

"If you're looking for an empowering, purposeful, and heartwarming read, you'll love this story. The first few pages reminded me of my own past and the four friends—Sage, Opti, Pessi, and Chill—helped me better understand my own behavior during challenging times. You'll relearn some fundamental lessons and discover how to deal with uncertainties—no matter how unexpected they are."

—Sinem Günel, entrepreneur, mentor, and fifteen-time top writer on
Medium.com

What Happens in Tomorrow World? is a creative, entertaining, and engaging fable that teaches you how to inspire each other and work together even when there is a gap in perspectives and opinions. I encourage you to savor each chapter, examine yourself, adhere to Sage's wisdom, and become your very best right where you are."

—David Cottrell, author of *Monday Morning Leadership* and
Quit Drifting, Lift the Fog, and Get Lucky

"A delightful parable with an important lesson for us all: 'I don't know what's going to happen. If I win, I win. If I lose, I lose. But, no matter what, I learn, I learn.' Life is about learning, we don't always win, it's the journey *that matters.*"

—Chester Elton, bestselling coauthor of *The Carrot Principle, Leading with Gratitude,* and *The Apostle of Appreciation*

What Happens in
TOMORROW
WORLD?

What Happens in
TOMORROW
WORLD?

• • •

A Modern-Day Fable About
Navigating Uncertainty

JORDAN GROSS

Matt Holt Books
An Imprint of BenBella Books, Inc.
Dallas, TX

BenBella Books, Inc.
10440 N. Central Expressway
Suite 800
Dallas, TX 75231
benbellabooks.com

Send feedback to feedback@benbellabooks.com

BenBella is a federally registered trademark.
Matt Holt and logo are trademarks of BenBella Books.

Printed in the United States of America
10 9 8 7 6 5 4 3 2 1

Library of Congress Control Number: 2020050369
ISBN 9781950665952 (print)
ISBN 9781953295187 (ebook)

Editing by Robb Pearlman
Copyediting by Michael Fedison
Proofreading by Lisa Story
Text design and composition by Katie Hollister
Cover design by Sarah Avinger
Illustrations by Ralph Voltz
Printed by Lake Book Manufacturing

Distributed to the trade by Two Rivers Distribution, an Ingram brand
www.tworiversdistribution.com

Dedicated to Grandpa David and Grandpa Morty.
The real-life Sage and Chill.

FOREWORD

Storytelling has always been at the forefront of the work I do. In my books and talks I share stories that touch the heart and lead to actions that create positive change. There is nothing like a good story to share lessons the reader will remember and apply to their life. I believe my audience feels connected to me because of the stories I share.

When a young, energetic, and eager up-and-coming author emailed me out of the blue about a TEDx talk he was giving on the power of creative storytelling in the personal development space, I felt compelled to answer. I gave him my phone number and he called me right away. This was the first time I talked to Jordan Gross. We chatted for about thirty minutes, and our discussion reaffirmed my mission and passion for writing business fables. Stories are fun to write and they connect with the reader at a deeper level. They open up the reader's mind to new and endless possibilities.

A few weeks later, I heard from Jordan again. To be quite honest, it wasn't a great time to hear from him. I was knee deep in promotion for a new fable I had written titled *The Garden.* I was hopping on webinars, doing podcast interviews, and assembling my launch team. Not to mention, it was at the very beginning of the coronavirus pandemic. To say it was a time of uncertainty would be an understatement.

This is why when Jordan mentioned he had written a parable about navigating uncertainty, I had to do something. Having overcome so much uncertainty in my life, I knew I wanted to encourage and support him in sharing this message.

This fun and entertaining story will help you move forward through times of uncertainty with optimism and power. It will make you laugh, smile, cry, and think about your own relationship with the varying degrees of uncertainty in your life and help you overcome challenges to create your future.

As you read the story, you will discover greater insight into yourself. Maybe you're Opti. Maybe you're Pessi. Maybe you're Sage. Maybe you're Chill. Yet, regardless of who you are, when there is uncertainty, there are two things I can say that matter most. First, pessimism will not move you forward. Second, faith, hope, and love for life and for others will move you forward to create the life you were born to live. I'm excited you are reading this—let's decide right now to move forward together.

—Jon Gordon, bestselling author of *The Energy Bus*, *The Carpenter*, and *The Garden*

"Embrace uncertainty. Some of the most beautiful chapters in our lives won't have a title until much later."

—Bob Goff

INTRODUCTION

I dropped everything when the coronavirus infiltrated our world. I wanted to be as helpful as possible to as many people as possible. So, I decided to write. I decided to share my emotions with my network, so they could realize they weren't the only ones feeling helpless. But I wasn't sure what to say. With so much uncertainty circulating in people's minds, I didn't know if what I wrote could actually make a difference.

But that's precisely it when it comes to uncertainty. We never know what's going to happen. We never know what's going to make a difference. But we must do our best to make others feel safe and loved anyway.

The magnitude of different events leads to varying levels of uncertainty, which in turn informs our responses. When considering what to share with my audience, I thought about some of the most uncertain times in my own life, and I assessed the way people around me reacted.

I was lucky enough to have grown up with all four of my grandparents—Grandpa Morty, Grandma Elly, Grandpa David, and Grandma Harriet. Until I was seventeen years old, I was smothered in tremendous bear hugs, bothered by lipstick-filled kisses, and graced with unparalleled wisdom. They were four very different, yet uniquely wonderful people, and I love and appreciate them more and more every day.

I used to see my grandparents pretty often, basically every month—for Jewish holidays, birthdays, anniversaries. Our small, yet tightly knit family would get together, most often at Grandma Harriet and Grandpa David's house in Queens, New York.

As the youngest grandchild, I would always sit on one of their laps as they talked about whatever was going on. Those conversations usually began with the weather.

You can learn a lot about somebody by asking them about the weather.

Someone once told me that the only difference between a day that's mostly sunny and partly cloudy is the weatherperson's mood.

We'd sit around the Friday night dinner table, and

somebody would inevitably ask about the forecast for the rest of the weekend. Each grandparent would play meteorologist.

"It's going to be a gorgeous weekend, just gorgeous," Grandma Harriet would say with her strong Brooklyn accent.

"What are you talking about, Harriet?" Grandma Elly would chime in. "High fifties and a 30 percent chance of showers is not gorgeous. It seems terrible to me."

Grandpa Morty went next. "What are you two yapping about? It's just weather. If it rains, wear a jacket. If it's warm, take it off. Who cares!"

Finally, they'd look at Grandpa David, always the last to speak. "We can't predict the weather, and it's out of our control, so why fuss over it? It may be sunny, or it may be cloudy. No matter what the weather may be, we can all still have a wonderful weekend together."

A couple years later, we were having another holiday dinner at that same dining room table at Grandma Harriet's house. I was in third grade, and Mrs. Tozar had just given me my first ever unsatisfactory mark on an essay. I showed up to Grandma's with a pout on my face, so naturally the topic of conversation that evening was *What's wrong with Jordan*?

I told them about my grade, and I explained how scared I was about all my writing assignments going forward. I had no idea if I'd ever get a good grade again.

Grandma Harriet started. "Aw, Jordan darling, don't worry about it. It's just one essay, and you are going to do beautifully on the next one!" I looked at her, glossy-eyed. "Ugh, you are just so delicious, I can't even get over it," she said.

Grandma Elly shared her own thoughts. "That's not good, Jordan. One bad grade can turn into two, and then who knows. You better be careful!"

"I was no good in school," Grandpa Morty would say. "It doesn't matter. Good grades, bad grades, who cares? Just move on, kid."

Grandpa David would speak last again after listening to all the other words of consolation. "Jordan, you are going to succeed, and you are going to fail. One isn't necessarily good and the other isn't necessarily bad. What matters most is what you learn from each experience."

Grandpa David and Grandma Harriet moved into an apartment by the time I was sixteen, but they still hosted all of our family gatherings.

Every Passover, the seder included a search for the *afikomen*. Traditionally, the eldest person, in this case Grandpa David, would hide a piece of matzah somewhere in the house, and then whichever kid found it won $20 and brag-ging rights until the next year. One Passover, my brother was away at Duke, so it was just me, my parents, and my four grandparents at dinner.

Since I was the only kid, I searched around the house, but I couldn't find the afikomen. I looked everywhere. When I finally gave up, we all asked Grandpa David to get it for me. We told him it was too good of a hiding spot. Smiling, he searched around the house, but he couldn't find it either. "Mice must have gotten it!" he joked to Grandma Harriet.

As we ate dessert, Grandma Elly mentioned something about the lost piece of matzah. "You know, it's not good that you forgot where you put the matzah, David—you should get yourself checked. Who knows what could be wrong with you? You may have a tumor!"

"God forbid, Elenore," Grandpa Morty responded. "So he lost the piece of stale bread. Who cares?" Grandpa Morty was not very religious.

"I'm sure he'll remember in a little bit! He always does; he'll find it!" Grandma Harriet said cheerfully.

Grandpa David was eating. He could sense all eyes were on him. "I'm sorry I lost it. I don't know if I'll find it soon. I don't know if I'll find it ever. All I know in this present moment is that this chocolate cake is mighty good!"

For the next few weeks, Grandpa David continued to

forget things. Keys here, cell phone there. He and Grandma Harriet decided to go to the doctor. Our family congregated for dinner shortly after.

As we started on dessert, Grandma Harriet spoke to me differently than she ever had before. She looked around the room. She placed her hand on top of mine.

"Jordan, dearest. Your grandpa David has Alzheimer's."

There was so much I wanted to say, so many questions I wanted to ask. But as water filled my eyes, all I managed to get out was, "So what's going to happen next?"

I obviously thought that, like clockwork, each grandparent would take their turn speaking. But to my surprise, Grandma Harriet did not say something positive. Grandma Elly did not say something negative. Grandpa Morty did not act with indifference. Grandpa David did not provide any sage advice.

Instead, nobody said a word. They just proceeded to get out of their chairs, circle around me, and give me the biggest, longest hug they could. Even the pessimistic Grandma Elly. The only response I heard was that we'd all get through this. With love and faith and support, we'd all get through this.

Maybe, during times of uncertainty, your behavior gravitates toward Grandma Elly. You're scared, nervous, and that makes you turn to facts. You become a realist, and that often comes off as negative and pessimistic.

Maybe you relate best to Grandma Harriet. You're an unshakeable optimist. No matter what happens, the future will be bright.

Or perhaps you're like Grandpa Morty. You're always cool and calm and collected. You don't take things too seriously, so you brush most of it off. You're often chill and indifferent.

And it's possible you're Grandpa David. You're spiritual, very much living in the present, not assigning all too much meaning to situations, good or bad.

But no matter which method resonates with you the most, there is no one correct response when you're faced with a situation that totally upends your world. There are no right answers. But there are wrong answers. And, as Grandma Elly realized, there is no place for pessimism and negativity during uncertain times.

And although no single response is best for every different level of uncertainty, the response that matters most is one that promotes hope and love and faith. It's about making the people around you who matter most feel safe. It's about making them feel loved. Just like my grandparents made me feel. Whether it's a hug, or some encouraging words, or no words at all, uncertainty is best faced together. Love and support are uncertainty's greatest adversaries.

As you immerse yourself in Tomorrow World and meet all of the characters within this magical arcade, think about how you've been reacting to the uncertainty in your life. Are you lifting up the people you love? Or are your fears and worries bringing you and others down? Which character or grandparent do you relate to the most? Is this really the person you want to be?

WHAT HAPPENS IN TOMORROW WORLD?

This is a story about a few magical toys in a magical arcade in a magical land called Cleveland. Just kidding. Cleveland is a real place, and it's actually pretty nice!

But what's not to kid about is this magical arcade called Tomorrow World and the wonderful things that happen within its four walls. One of Tomorrow World's most remarkable machines is the giant crane game called *What's Next?!* And inside this machine are four lively, animated stuffed toys:

Pessi—a frowning blobfish
Chill—a laid-back but sometimes cold smoothie
Sage—a wise old robot
Opti—a confident lioness

Two gargantuan statues of red question marks, one upside down, one right side up, flank the left and right sides of the tinted glass doors of Tomorrow World. Children often climb, sit, and stand on them while their parents take pictures.

Above the glass doors is a sign that in sometimes purple, sometimes red, or sometimes blue letters reads, "Tomorrow World," flashing one letter at a time, always in a random order. Under the arcade's name in smaller letters is the phrase, "What will tomorrow bring?"

Once the automatic glass doors slide apart, visitors are greeted by two wide, vibrant tunnels, which block their view of most of the rest of the arcade. If they go right, colorful pinball machines surround glow-in-the-dark air hockey tables. Skee-Ball lanes sit beside Dance Dance Revolution stages. And to the left, there are electronic slot machines (giving out tickets, not money), kid-sized race cars, convertibles, boats, and airplanes.

A prominent feature, visible to all from the front entrance, is the wonderful wall of prizes. Thousands of prizes line the back wall of Tomorrow World. At the top of the wall of prizes is a tinted window with a sign on it that reads, "The Big Boss." Shadows of various shapes and sizes come and go throughout the day, but nobody can pinpoint which figure the boss really is. Only Dana, the cheerful game operator and floor manager, interacts with the big boss, and she has taken an oath never to reveal her identity until something totally out of the ordinary happens.

There are luscious smells coming from an adjacent cafeteria where burgers, hot dogs, fries, and chicken fingers are ubiquitous, each meal accompanied by a small toy, to the delight of every guest. Most kids, however, opt for the mystery box—an assortment of different snacks sure to sate their appetites.

Tomorrow World is a special place with so many entertaining games and activities inside. But there is one game that consistently draws the most people and the longest lines, one place where whispers can be heard from the opposite end of the arcade.

The *What's Next?!* giant crane game.

Set smack-dab in the center of the floor is a glass display larger than most bedrooms. Enormous metal claws hang from the top of the ceiling, ready to drop as soon as contestants find the prize they most desire. When contestants hit the DROP! button, there's no turning back. The claws slowly lower and widen, and just as they hit the target, the claws cave inward, attempting to grasp whatever's within reach! If they pick up a toy, the player gets to go again and try for the *What's Next Challenge*, in which if a player can capture three toys in a row, then they get a fourth toy of their choosing. If not, then each person gets a consolation prize from Dana, the former high school cheerleader turned machine operator there to commentate, get contestants to scream, "What's Next?!" to constantly promote the game, and support each person who dares to play. Nobody knows if they'll win, yet everybody still comes to give it a try. This game has the best toys, the best prizes, and the best over-all experience, but it's also the most challenging. Kids from around the world play, day in and day out.

On the top of the glass is the game's name, *What's Next?!*, in neon green letters, and underneath is the phrase "Where anything can happen!" The rest of the design is simple, except for a phrase in teeny tiny writing on the left-hand corner just beside where contestants insert their coins to play. It's a phrase so small that oftentimes people don't even see it. It reads, "You always get a prize." But to the toys inside, it just looks like gibberish.

For the longest time, nobody had ever even come close to winning the *What's Next Challenge*—until Catch Alltoys came along.

efore we get to Catch, though, we must first talk about some of these amazingly wonderful, wickedly awesome characters inside of the *What's Next?!* crane game. There are lions and tigers and bears, and a surprised face emoji that says, "Oh, my!" There are board games to win, video games to play, and game consoles to snag.

But perhaps the hardest to grab, because of the nature of the material, their odd shapes, and unique sizes, are four of the oldest toys in the game, who have seen almost everything from their central vantage point.

Pessi, the frowning blobfish. Chill, the laid-back, sometimes overly cold smoothie. Sage, the seemingly programmed, yet wise old robot. And Opti, the confident, upbeat lioness.

Pessi lies underneath a mountain of other objects on the bottom left corner of the prize container. That's where she started, and that's where she stays. She's pink and bubbly with a round nose, piercing black eyes, and T-Rex-shaped fins at her sides. But what's most noticeable about Pessi is the incessant frown she wears across her face.

Chill's cylindrical shape alternates between aqua blue and cherry red. He has an orange swirl coming out of the top of the cylinder crowned with a white bendy straw. On the front and back of his cup is his name, "Chill," in bubble letters. Chill started out in the middle of the toys, but he's moved all over since. The crane always has a way of moving him everywhere, but he never seems to mind.

Then there's Sage. Sage is a pretty standard robot—rectangular silver head, circular eyes and ears, box-shaped body. Sage began his journey on the top right-hand side of the plethora of toys, and although he may move around throughout the day, something almost always brings him back to that spot. Something about it just feels right.

Lastly, there's Opti. Opti is the fiercest, most powerful, most noticeable doll in all of the *What's Next?!* game. She has piercing green eyes, pearly white fangs, chestnut fur, and the long, thin tail of a lioness. She is placed front and center in the display for all to see. Almost half of the participants use their first attempt to try and grab Opti, but to no avail. Opti remains confident, powerful, and content in her place at the center of the toy jungle.

It's mid-March, just approaching the spring equinox. Cleveland is experiencing the kind of weather that's neither good nor bad. It's neither hot nor cold. It can be raining part of the day with high winds, and then all of a sudden, the sun will poke its head out and reward Clevelanders with sixty-degree warmth. It's one of those times of year when you question why being a meteorologist is actually even a thing, because they've been wrong four days in a row now. The weather outside is so difficult to predict that not even four mystical dolls can decide what to make of it.

"Looks like a beautiful day out there, doesn't it? I can see the sun just above those buildings! And, yay! I see people without jackets! Wow, it must be amazing to be outside!" Opti glistens as she presses her face up against the glass.

"I appreciate and admire your positivity, Opti. And if today the weather is supposed to be beautiful, then it shall be beautiful. But if it is not, then it is not. We cannot control this. I have faith that no matter the weather, people will still have a wonderful day if they believe that there is a wonderful day to be had," Sage says as he peers at all of his fellow toys and games, ready to approach whatever's next.

"I don't know—I just don't really care about the weather, I guess. It's fine, it's okay, but it's just weather, ya know?" Chill says as he stretches out his bendy straw and lets out a yawn. Opti intervenes.

"Chill, why doesn't the weather excite you? There are so many possibilities! It can be sunny. It can be rainy. It can be foggy, misty, you-y."

"You-y?" Chill asks.

"CHILLY!" Opti roars with a large smirk. "I just think sometimes you have to care a bit more about things that really matter because—"

"CLOUD! CLOOOOOOOOUUUUUUUUD! Oh, my goodness, I see a cloud, and then there's another one, and there's one over there. That's three clouds in the sky now, oh no, no, no, it is not going to be a beautiful day. I just don't think so. And oh my, my, what are those? It can't be. This isn't happening. This is not happening!" Pessi speaks over her pals with little concern or awareness.

Opti looks over at Pessi. "What is it, Pessi?" she says, lovingly.

"SWEATPANTS. I see sweatpants." Pessi points her

little fin and taps the glass a few times for emphasis. Her black eyes widen.

"Relax, Pessi, they're just sweatpants," Chill says with an eye roll.

Then Opti chimes in. "Pessi, sweatpants can be a good thing! Maybe that person just had a sporting event? Maybe that person prefers to keep their legs warm? Maybe that person hasn't had much sun yet this year, so they want to keep those pale legs away from people! And three clouds? That's nothing! The other day you said there were twelve clouds, and we still heard everyone saying how beautiful it was outside, remember?"

"How can you be so sure, Opti? I am just observing the facts!" Pessi pleads. "Three clouds have turned into three hundred, sweatpants have been accompanied by snow boots, one day of bad weather has led to many more. I just can't even imagine this. It's too much. It's going to be another bad day. This is for certain."

"Pessi, stop it! You just have to think positively. You just gotta! It's better for you!" Opti says.

Sage begins to chuckle and speaks. "There may be sweatpants and there may be clouds. There may not be sun and there may not be jackets. What is important, however, is not to give meaning to whether or not one or the other is too good or too bad. Some may prefer cold weather while others may like it warm. Some may like to wear sweatpants while some may like shorts. What is most important to remember is that we must not judge. We must never judge others, right, Chill?"

"Right," Chill says. Another eye roll.

"And we mustn't try to get others to always agree with our perspective, right, Opti?"

"Yes, of course!" Opti says enthusiastically.

"And we don't make the future any better or worse by worrying about it so much. Our worries have no influence over what is bound to happen. Isn't that so, Pessi?"

"I . . . I guess that makes sense, Sage." Pessi pauses. "But I still don't think it's going to be a nice day!"

"Yes, it will be!" Opti erupts.

"You both gotta take it down like ten notches. My head is killing me. It's just weather, let it be!" Chill moans.

Sage sits atop all the prizes in his back-right corner. He breathes audibly as the automatic sliding doors open, welcoming the first wave of children into Tomorrow World.

As the children run around Tomorrow World figuring out what games they want to play first, Opti, Pessi, Sage, and Chill can feel a different aura in the arcade. They can see the children whispering in one another's ears. They're up on their tippy-toes looking around for something, or possibly someone. In the distance, the toys can hear a conversation between Dana and one of the children. It's a conversation they've heard before.

"She's coming! She's coming! Today is the day she'll be here! This is such a happy day!" Opti rages with joy.

"Who's coming? Actually, don't answer that. It doesn't really matter to me," Chill remarks.

"I don't think she's coming today. Why would she come today of all days? We have heard that she was coming before, and she didn't come, so I believe today will be no different. But, then again, if she does come, then we are doomed! But I don't think she will come. But when she doesn't come, it's still a bad thing because then we will just have to wait longer for when she does come! There are no good scenarios." Pessi's frown widens.

Sage speaks to Pessi and Opti. "Opti, Pessi, we don't know if she will come or not. We cannot predict one way or another, so we must not let it impact how we feel in the present moment. Our expectations and attachment to these expectations are what cause us stress and anxiety. When we relinquish this attachment to an outcome, we are liberated from any sort of devastation no matter the result."

"OK, I normally wouldn't ask, but now I'm curious," Chill chimes in. "Who are we talking about?"

"Catch Alltoys!" Pessi and Opti say in unison, yet with very different tones of voice.

"Don't you remember hearing all about Catch Alltoys, Chill?" Opti questions. "We have heard a bunch of stories over the last few months and years about her!"

"Not really. Remind me if you'd like. Doesn't really matter to me," Chill states.

Opti begins excitedly: "So, legend has it that a new mother was holding her baby girl in her right arm and fumbling around for her house keys with her left. After a minute of searching, she got frustrated, and thrust her key chain out of her pocket, forcing it to fly high up into the air. Mom went for the keys, but just barely missed the grab.

But, as if in slow motion, the keys fell effortlessly into the outstretched hands of the beautiful baby girl cradled by her mother's right arm. It was in that moment that Cayla Alltoys got her nickname. 'Catch.'"

Opti is interrupted by screams from the bottom of the toy pile.

"Wait, wait, wait!" It's Pessi. "Doubt it! I am not buying that story, Opti. There is no way a baby could catch that key chain without getting hurt! The keys probably fell and hit the ground, and everybody just wants to make it seem like this Cayla Alltoys is so great at catching! No baby can catch. Nobody is that great at catching. Nobody ever wants to catch me. But I don't want to be caught anyway."

To this, Chill replies, "Why does it matter if the story is true or not, Pessi? Just let it be what it is."

"I will agree with Chill," Sage says. "But I will phrase it slightly differently. The story may be true, and it may be false. But we cannot let the outcome of the story impact how we feel. It mustn't change our mood. Now, Opti, you seemed so excited, so why don't you continue your story?"

Opti gives Sage an air hug and reveals more about the myth of Catch Alltoys.

"For the next few years, baby Catch caught everything. Her parents would toss her food and she'd catch it in her mouth. They tossed her stuffed animals, and she caught those too. One time, her dad even dropped a donut he was eating, which landed perfectly on Catch's tiny baby toes.

"As Catch grew up, she excelled at sports. She caught baseballs with a first-base mitt. She caught footballs as the oversized helmet shielded her eyes. She caught soccer balls with big funny goalie gloves. She hated sports like volleyball, tennis, and golf, because there was nothing to catch!

"One Saturday afternoon, Catch and her family went to a local diner in Columbus, Ohio. They went to this diner all the time, but there was something different about it. There were kids in the waiting area, and it looked like they were having fun! How could that be?

"When Catch finally squeezed her way through the crowd and made it to the front, her jaw dropped as quickly and as far down as the claw did in the crane game in front of her. It was something new for her to catch!

"As each kid took their turn and tried to get the different prizes in the diner's newest attraction, Catch watched carefully. She analyzed the speed of the drop, the dimensions of the claws, the shapes and sizes of the toys inside. She saw face after face go from smile to frown, as each participant's mindset went from hope to despair. She asked her dad for a quarter, which would give her one shot at the crane game in the waiting room of the diner."

"Hold it right there!" Pessi shouts. "You're telling me

a little kid was analyzing drop speed and claw dimensions? Come on, Opti, you know that's not true! There is no way that happened. This story is bogus!"

"Pessi, please do not rush to conclusions and interrupt. Allow Opti to finish the story," Sage insists.

Chill says nothing. He just casually blows a bubble out of his straw.

Opti proceeds.

"Catch waited her turn in line and watched each kid drop the crane into a pool of toys and come up with nothing. She heard kids complain that it was rigged, that nobody would ever win. Finally, after the girl in front of her came up short and wished her luck, it was Catch's turn.

"Catch looked at her mom and dad, gave her dad a firm handshake and a fist bump (their secret shake), and said to them, 'I don't know what's going to happen. If I win, I win. If I lose, I lose. But, no matter what, I learn, I learn.' Her soccer coach taught her that one. She placed the quarter into the crane game.

"Catch could smell the minty freshness of the peppermint patties inside the game. She could feel the sweat droplets accumulating on her forehead. She placed her right pointer finger on the *Forward* arrow first. The crane jolted. She took a deep breath. She tapped *Forward* three more times. The crane swayed back and forth vigorously. She

29

waited. Then she tapped *Right* five times quickly. She waited again. She stepped away from the machine. She walked to the right side of it. Then the left. She pressed the *Backward* button one time. She waited for the crane to stop swaying. Then she slammed her palm on the red DROP! button. The crane opened its claws wide and swooped downward ferociously, at first grabbing everything in its path. Then, it began to tighten. As candy, dolls, gadgets, and gizmos fell back into the pile, one item remained. The crane dropped it into the prize box, and Catch took it out and looked at the mini soccer ball she wanted. The other kids stared at her wide-eyed as she trotted out of the diner with her folks.

"For the next year, whenever the Alltoyses would go to the diner, Catch would play the crane game, and she would win. She would win whatever she wanted in the entire display case. She even became sort of an urban legend in the area, and anytime kids saw her at the diner, they would ask her to win their favorite toy for them. She agreed, but she assured them of the same thing every single time she played: *I don't know what's going to happen. If I win, I win. If I lose, I lose. But, no matter what, I learn, I learn.*"

"Stop, stop, stop!" Pessi shrieks. "Catch sounds completely perfect, platonically good, and emotionally zen. How? No single-digit child acts that way!"

"Again, Pess, doesn't matter. It's a story," Chill retorts.

"It's true!" Opti screams.

Sage looks at them and sniffles once before speaking. "We mustn't let doubt cloud our judgment of situations. It should not skew our perceptions of people. Catch may be all of these things, and she may not. Maybe she does not make mistakes, but maybe she also does. Maybe she has not yet experienced trauma that may actually make her break away from these seemingly infallible characteristics. We just cannot be so sure, so we just cannot judge. Please finish telling us about this mysterious character, Opti."

Opti is glad to finish.

"Anyway, one day, after wrapping up a round of getting prizes for others, Catch decided to play a round for herself. There was an intriguing piece of paper rolled up and tied with a thin red ribbon. Catch wanted that, and after doing her usual ritual, this is exactly what Catch caught.

"She untied the ribbon and unrolled the paper like a sacred scroll. The prize was an invitation from Dana and the big boss upstairs to come here to Tomorrow World and try to win us! Catch is our ticket out of this place, so we can embark on a new adventure, no matter what happens next!"

Opti concludes her story with a twinkle in her eye,

optimistic and excited for the future. Pessi flubs her lips and continues to frown. Chill sits unfazed. And Sage thanks Opti for her story, and he assures his friends that no matter what happens, they will be able to handle it together.

As soon as the Tomorrow World doors open, Dana begins to line the kids (and some adults!) up single file, an impressive display of humanity that stretches back at least a quarter of a football field. Each player is here for the *What's Next Challenge.* One chance. One drop. Get a prize, keep going. Get nothing, you're done!

Dana usually takes a good ten minutes lining people up before the first participant of the day gives it their best shot. This gives the prizes inside some time to chat. Pessi begins to worry.

"What do you guys think is going to happen today? Ah, there is just so much uncertainty! Do we get scooped up? Do we not get scooped up? Do we move around? Chill, you always get moved around, so I guess that'll happen. Aren't you afraid? I heard there will be two thousand people here today. More than two thousand chances for us to leave our home! How are you all not freaking out right now? The day is about to begin and at any moment we can be in Tomorrow

World! Like real Tomorrow World, not just inside of *What's Next?!* You all should be more scared. Who's to say what's on the other side?"

"I'm actually pumped up for today, Pessi!" Opti says as she puts on her widest grin, revealing her sharp pearly whites for all the gamers to see. "I think Tomorrow World is great, and I'd be excited to see what was outside of here. I just know I'm gonna get out there someday. I just know it!"

"Just another day to me. No big deal, you know how it is," Chill says with a cold look toward Pessi and then Opti. "What are your thoughts?" Chill looks toward Sage.

"Today is another opportunity to be present. We must not look too much into what we want or expect to happen in the future, because it is then that we will not enjoy living right now. I know that if any of us get chosen today to leave this place, there will be a good reason for it. And if we do not, then there is a reason for that as well."

As Sage finishes his sentence, the flashing lights of the game begin to sound, and Dana begins her words of direction and encouragement.

"Alrighty then, what's your name, strong guy? Ira? Glad to meet ya, Ira. Why don't you step right up here for me in front of the big red trampoline-looking button that says DROP!? Now, Ira, you are participating in the *What's Next Challenge*, so you get one chance to grab a prize. If you get one, you go again, but if not, you get one of those awesome consolation prizes. Sound good to you? Alright, elbow tap, and let's get this day going! Can you tell me, Ira, what's next?!" Dana asks this question to all participants. The kids always know what to say back.

With that, Ira screams, "I'm gonna get new video games!" and he runs to the button that says *Right*, and he jumps on it two times. Then he scurries over to the one that says *Forward*, and he stomps it down four times. Then he pushes *Backward* once. And finally, he jumps with his two feet onto the big red trampoline-looking button that says DROP! The giant claw pauses for a second, and then, just like the big drop on a roller coaster, dives hastily into the prizes.

"Noooooooooooooooooooo!" Pessi screams. The metal tongs graze Opti's tail, but she is otherwise unscathed. Sage sits comfortably in his corner, as does Pessi in hers. But where's Chill? Along with a tablet, a gigantic purple zebra, and a few video games, Chill is in the crane's almighty grip! But just as the crane makes a turn to the prize tube, all the items fall out, leaving poor Ira with nothing. He runs away with his head in his palms, forgetting to snag his consolation prize.

The magical pals have survived the first run of the day.

"That was a close call, wasn't it, you guys?! Chill, we

could have lost you! It's just terrible. Every new person who jumps on that button presents another moment that can change our lives forever! It can change our lives for the worse!" Pessi speaks quickly and nervously.

"Or the better!" Opti replies.

Nobody speaks. Then Chill breaks the silence. "Don't look at me, I couldn't care less about what happens." He pauses and looks at Sage. "Isn't it about time for your pre-programmed words of wisdom?"

Sage stares out the window toward the other prizes on the back wall. "You know, Chill, there is a difference between not caring and not fearing what happens next. Not caring represents indifference, which is a grave danger, because with indifference, there are no solutions. There is no action. But not fearing, and please listen up here, Pessi. Not fearing and being open to whatever happens next, well, then you get to have a say in what happens next, because it'll be fully based on how you respond. Things are going to happen one way or another. And even if you are 99.99 percent sure they will turn out a certain way, there is always that .01 percent chance that they will not. Not fearing the .01 percent and even being prepared for the .01 percent is where learning and growth occurs. It's how you build strength, character, and it's how you move forward no matter the adversity."

"But I listen all the time to the conversations about

the outside world!" Pessi retorts. "They talk about viruses wiping out populations, climate change that is dooming the world, economic collapses, people hurting other people, not to mention what the kids are always talking about . . ." She stops.

"Talking about what?" Opti urges.

"HOMEWORK. I do not want to do homework, Sage. That sounds just awful!"

Opti responds to Pessi. "Well, I only listen to the good conversations. The ones in which people are laughing, kids are talking about winning their sports games, acing their tests. I just surround myself with all that kinda stuff, and it keeps me feeling great! And then I try my best to share that info with you guys!" Opti says excitedly.

Chill's turn. "I don't listen to anything. It's all noise. If I hear it, I hear it. If I don't, I don't. I try not to get too bogged down or think about too much, especially if it doesn't affect me."

Sage finally shares his perspective. "You are all able to feel how you want to feel, and you may act how you want to act. It is your life, after all. But if I may, can I enable you to consider something about each of your perspectives?"

"As long as it doesn't make me feel worse," Pessi says.

"Right on!" Opti shouts.

"You're going to share anyway," Chill asserts.

"Well, Pessi, do you think that listening to all of these negative conversations is helping you at all? Do you believe it's helping others? Or perhaps it's only making things worse for you, convincing you that this is all that is out there, obstructing you from having any faith that things can be good. The more you surround yourself with negativity, the more news you consume, the more likely you are to stay stuck in your ways that are not serving you in the best way possible. Do you like feeling this down all the time, Pessi? I don't believe you do. So, maybe not listening so much and not sharing the negative information you do hear with others—maybe that will help everyone?"

"I can try, I guess."

"Opti, positivity is a good thing, a very good thing, but it is just one tool. It is not the only answer. You have to be respectful of people you love like Pessi, who don't necessarily have the ability just yet to always think like you do. If you solely surround yourself with the positive, then you become unaware of pain. And the goal of our lives, Opti—although many may believe the opposite—is not to hide from pain, but rather to learn from it. So, yes, listen to these uplifting conversations, but maybe try to not be so singularly focused. Allow other thoughts to flow through your mind and see how those thoughts make you feel as well. It will help you understand better how to make an impact on your friends."

"You got it, dude!" Opti raises her paw emulating a thumbs-up.

"And, Chill, my good friend Chill. I think you have an understanding of how we should react to the uncertainties in this world, but you are too afraid to relinquish your ego, to self-sabotage your unfazed persona, and to admit to yourself that you have the ability to truly help others. If you just make one little shift, if you realize that being calm and 'chill' as you call it is not about indifference and pushing away the unknown, but rather, it's about embracing the unknown and inviting it into your life, then you will be able to lead those like Opti and Pessi. You mention that you do not get bogged down by things that do not impact you, which is a fine start, but what about your loved ones? Don't you want them to thrive as well? Don't you want them to do better, be better, be more prepared for what's next? For them to be prepared when anything can happen? For them to be content in Tomorrow World, no matter what tomorrow brings?"

Chill doesn't respond.

"I believe you do, Chill. I believe you do."

A drop of smoothie trickles down Chill's cup like he just watched the final scene of a romantic comedy, but he quickly wipes it away. He is glad he is in the middle of the prizes where nobody can see how he really feels.

For the next few hours, child after child, and a few

39

adults, too, jump on that DROP! button. And although the prizes shift around and it seems their lives out in the real Tomorrow World may begin, the four pals fall from the crane at the last second, able to return to comfort, to normalcy, for another attempt.

That is, until Catch Alltoys came along.

From Pessi's position at the bottom of the toys, she is able to see through the glass and into the parking lot. She often keeps her eyes away from all the people coming in and out of the arcade, but sometimes her eyes can't resist, and she is stunned at the potential danger of the cars, the sliding glass doors, and the crowds of people. At 2 PM, Pessi's eyes zero in on a family outside, and she decides to tell the rest of the group.

"Everyone! I see something outside!"

"What is it?" Opti asks.

"There's always something outside, you just never look," Chill asserts.

"Would you like to share with us what you see?" Sage offers.

"I see a girl and her mom and dad. And she's wearing a backwards cap. She's blowing bubbles with her chewing gum. Oh my, I hope she doesn't swallow it! I heard that will live inside of her for seven years if she swallows it!

41

"Anyway, the girl just hopped in the upside-down question mark, and her mom joined her for a picture. The dad's finger was blocking the camera, I guess, so they had to take the picture twice. She gave her parents a big hug, she did some sort of secret handshake with her dad, and now she's just staring at the sliding glass doors. What is she looking at? It's terrifying!"

"She's probably just looking," Chill states matter-of-factly.

"I think she's excited! I know I would be excited if I were coming to Tomorrow World!" Opti yells.

"I am not sure what she is looking at. None of us can be. But from the looks of the kids around the arcade, I feel like this may be a big day. This may be a special player entering our world," Sage says as he looks around and sees the children gossiping about the player ready to come inside.

Catch Alltoys tugs on her parents' arms as she skips over to the *What's Next?!* giant crane game. She acts mature for a nine-year-old, but she's still a kid who has finally arrived in an arcade.

Catch looks at the long line of people waiting their turn to play the game. Then she walks up to the front of the glass and stares directly into Opti's huge green eyes. Catch lights up. She looks at the rest of the prizes inside. She walks around to the left side, assessing the dimensions, the shapes, the feel of the toys within. She sees the velocity of the crane, its stability, its sturdiness. She assesses where and when the prizes fall out most often as she waits and watches a few turns. She walks behind the glass box and again makes eye contact with Opti, but she relinquishes her awe for this mighty toy. She must focus on the task at hand—three catches in a row. She watches one more try from behind the chamber to see if she notices anything different, but she thinks she has it all figured out. She then walks to the right side of the box and peers inside one last time to see if there are any exceptional prizes she wants. In that moment, she's not staring at him, but he's staring at her.

Sage notices something unique about the girl looking into *What's Next?!* He can feel something different about her. He can feel that something magical is about to happen.

"Why is she looking at us like that? Why is she walking around like that? Did we do something wrong? Did I do something wrong?" Pessi frets.

"Whoa, that girl seems cool, and I like her! I hope if anyone gets me out of here today, it's her! She would make a really amazing owner!" Opti replies.

"Whatever," Chill slurps.

"There is something different about this one," Sage ponders. "This is somebody who thinks. This is somebody who considers all options. This is somebody who understands preparation and intentional design. She realizes the uncertainty of the game, but she does her best to maximize everything that is within her control. And I have a feeling that she is content knowing that there are things outside of her control as well. She is here to learn, not just to win, and this is why I believe she is different."

"Oh no, different isn't good!" Pessi shouts.

"Different can be good!" Opti hollers back.

"This is like my sixth brain freeze of the day. You guys gotta tone it down," says Chill.

Sage sighs audibly again. Then he looks at the prizes on the back wall. He is almost certain things are about to change.

When Catch finishes her examination of *What's Next?!*
Dana immediately realizes who she is. She welcomes
her with open arms.

"You must be Catch Alltoys! We heard you like to take
a look around at things before playing for your prizes. You
are quite the legend around here, little missy! Not many
Columbus folks make a name for themselves in Cleveland
before even getting here! So, are you ready to go? I've been
told to give you the fastest pass we have, which allows you to
skip that insane line for the *What's Next Challenge*! So, what
do you say? Want to step right up?"

"Hi, yea, I'm Catch," she says shyly. "And I'm not that
good. I can miss a catch just like everybody else, but thanks
for saying that. I'm actually a little hungry. It's been a long
drive. Do you have any food?"

"Do we have any food?!" Dana sarcastically questions.
"Not only do we have food, but also the chef prepared you

a mystery box! Why don't you go enjoy some lunch with your parents, and then come back to me whenever you're ready? Deal?"

"Deal." Catch smiles.

"Elbows!" Dana points her elbow toward Catch. Catch bumps her elbow and then heads to the cafeteria portion of Tomorrow World.

As the Alltoyses eat, Catch tells her parents about being offered to cut the whole line to attempt the *What's Next Challenge*.

"That is quite a nice gesture, sweetie! Why don't you seem excited?"

"I just feel like you can't rush things like this. Especially when I don't know how things are going to end up, I don't want to go or make a decision too quickly. I want to take my time. I want to see how everyone else is doing. I want to learn a bit more, maybe talk to some of the kids while I wait. And also, I don't want to seem like I have special treatment, because then I feel like I may be resented. Why should I get treated any differently than anyone else? We are all in the same situation. We all have the same chance of winning or losing. We are all here trying to have fun at Tomorrow World, so I don't want it to seem like I have a leg up on anyone. We're all just human beings at the end of the day, and we should be treated equally!"

Catch's parents put their arms around each other, and through glossy eyes say together, "What did we do to get such a special girl?"

They finish up their lunch and Catch skips over to Dana, thanking her for allowing her to cut, but ultimately saying that she wants to wait in line just like everybody else. She knows the kids are looking at her, talking about her, but she doesn't want any extra attention. Dana gives Catch another elbow tap and goes back to cheering on the next contestant.

Sage doesn't often listen to conversations, but he hears every word of this one. His intuition is tingling.

As she waits in line and watches, Catch hears whispers and receives stares from the other kids, and even from some adults.

"That's Catch Alltoys from Columbus! I heard she's never dropped a toy in her life!" one girl says.

"I've heard she's never dropped *anything* in her life!" a boy corrects. Another one says, "I heard she is so good, she's cleared out an entire crane game without any drops. I bet she can catch a fish straight out of the water with her bare hands!"

"I bet she can catch me a new husband," a woman mumbles under her breath.

Catch watches and listens, watches and listens. She talks to the girl ahead of her, who's here attempting the *What's Next Challenge* for the seventh time this week! She's lost track of how many times she's tried overall. Her name is Ani, and she tells Catch that, at this point, she just wants any of the prizes from inside *What's Next?!* She's tired of the consolation prizes. But, if she had to choose, she'd probably pick the robot in the back, because her mom is an inventor, and she wants to give it to her.

When it's finally Ani's turn, Catch wishes her luck and gives her a pointer to wait an extra second before jumping on the DROP! button. But Ani doesn't listen. Her crane comes up empty. She grabs her consolation prize and walks away, shoulders drooped.

After two hours of waiting in line, Catch Alltoys is ready to take on the *What's Next Challenge*.

Dana introduces her loudly. "Ladies and gentlemen, boys and girls. We have a very, very special challenger here today with us. She is the queen of quality grabs. She is the princess of prizes. She is the damsel without a drop. Joining us all the way from Columbus, Ohio, it's Caaaaaaaaatch All-toys!!!!! Catch was invited here after finding a secret letter we sent to her local crane game machine at her favorite diner. That's right, Catch, we knew you'd grab that scroll and make your way down to Tomorrow World! Anyway, we are so excited to have you, and without further ado, Whaaaaaaaat's Next?!"

"The *What's Next Challenge*?" Catch says shyly.

"What was that?" Dana screams.

"The *What's Next Challenge*!" Catch says, louder now.

"Are there any words you'd like to say before you begin, Catch?" Dana asks.

Catch walks up to her dad, shakes his hand, and fist bumps. She hugs her mom's waist. Then she walks back up to Dana and announces, into the microphone, "I don't know what's going to happen. If I win, I win. If I lose, I lose. But, no matter what, I learn, I learn."

And with that, the music starts to play and the game begins.

Sage addresses his friends delicately.

"I want you all to know that we may soon experience the greatest uncertainty we have ever faced. This girl may guide us toward unprecedented waters. But our lives are never certain anyway. We have an illusion of certainty based on the safety we experience, the lack of change, the clinging on to what we believe to be true. But now, this illusion of certainty may change, and I just want you to be prepared. During such uncertain times, it is our preparation that shines brightest. We fall back onto the very core of our actions, routines, and beliefs. This is where one's truest persona reveals itself. How will you reveal yourself? Please consider this."

Sage again looks toward the prize wall. Then he looks at the consolation prizes, and finally he looks at Ani. She's watching, waiting with her consolation prize in hand. Sage nods his head.

"Who would you become if everything changed?" he says aloud.

"I would be the best version of me! I would be upbeat and enthusiastic and push others to be the best versions of themselves too! Gosh, I hope I get that chance. I hope she wins me!" Opti says.

"I can't really say. I don't have any facts to go off of. That is such a scary question. I don't even want to think about it!" Pessi shrieks, her frown elongating.

Chill doesn't respond. He just quietly considers, exactly as Sage had asked.

Catch knew which prize she wanted first. She had locked eyes with it while staring at the front and back of the four glass walls. Honestly, even while waiting for her turn, she barely took her eyes off of the enchanting lioness in the front center of the window.

The crane starts off right in the center of *What's Next?!*, so it seems all Catch has to do is step on the *Backward* button five times for it to line up perfectly with Opti. Most often, the prizes against the wall are the hardest to snag. But Catch realizes that the trick is to shift once to the left or right of the toy on the wall she wants, because then the claw would scoop it up and bring it in, as opposed to just collapse on top of it. It allows a chance for other toys to be collected as well.

Catch calmly walks to the center and stands in front of the DROP! button. It's important to let the crane stop swaying, so it can drop optimally, just as she'd told Ani to do. As she waits for it to stop, she looks around the room at the hundreds of eyes on her. She can hear the cheers. She can smell the cotton candy, the popcorn, and the sweat dripping off of her fellow adolescents. The machine stops. Catch jumps.

The crane swoops down like a hawk as she slams on the button.

"Noooooooo!" Pessi yelps.

Three items are swooped up immediately. The lioness, an oversized doll, and a third that Catch can't see because the two others are blocking her view. The crane rises up to the top of the glass, and then it jerks its way over to the prize drop box. Catch realizes that most of the toys fall at the turn before the final drop, so although some are already applauding, she waits patiently. And as she suspected, the oversized doll falls from the sky, knocking Opti down with it, sneaking through the crane's grasp. But there is still one toy left.

It's Chill! He lies motionless, cradled by the crane like a baby. And then, he falls swiftly into an unfamiliar box. Dana walks over to the bin and excitedly screams, "We have a winner!!! Congratulations, Catch, you are one for one! This is one of the oldest toys we have in Tomorrow World, Chill the Smoothie! Are you ready to go again?"

While it's not the lioness she wanted, Catch Alltoys got something from that round she needed even more: She learned.

"So close to getting me! I know she's gonna try again! She missed me by just a hair! But I am so glad she was able to scoop up Chill. That is amazing—what a reward!" Opti says.

"Chill is gone. Nothing will ever be the same. I'm gonna miss his bendy straw so much. If Chill can be gone, then you guys can be gone next. Then I'll be all alone. Nobody will ever pick me. I'm just a blob in the bottom left-hand corner of a world filled with joy. I am not joy. I do not bring joy. Nobody wants something that does not bring joy." Pessi sinks lower and frowns more than ever.

"Don't say that! People do want you!" Opti objects.

"Pessi, these are words that come from somebody who has lost faith. These are words that come from somebody who wants others to feel sorry for her. These are words that come from somebody who wants to feel sorry for herself. These are words that come from somebody who is stagnant during times of uncertainty. But, most importantly, these are words that come from somebody who is not you. This is not who you are or want to be, Pessi. I know you have it in you to not spread negativity and feel sorry for yourself." Sage tries to look at Pessi, but she is facing the other way.

Tears stream down from her dark eyes.

just need a second before I try for round two," Catch says. She then walks slowly around the entire glass box, fixating on the left side. She squats down, tilts her head, and smiles at the frowning face looking back at her.

"Perfect," she whispers.

"I'm ready," Catch tells Dana.

"OK, then, so Whaaaaat's Next?!"

"The *What's Next Challenge*!" Catch screams. The lights begin to flicker, and the music plays. Catch coolly walks over to the *Left* button and steps on it until the crane bangs up against the wall. Then she presses *Forward* three times. She waits for the swaying to come to a halt.

After Catch's last attempt, she realizes she has to shake up her strategy. Sadly, Opti's shape is not conducive to this style of crane, and given Opti had moved a bit because of the last try, Catch doesn't want to take the risk. But there is one prize that she notices has an excellent shape. It's just in a difficult spot in the bottom left corner of the box. Catch figures most kids don't try for the toy because it doesn't look as fun as all the others, but she really likes the little fish. She actually believes her round shape would be a perfect fit for this crane.

Once the claw finishes moving, Catch skips off of one foot and lands on the mega-sized DROP! button.

"Noooooooo!" Pessi yelps, as per usual. But it is too late. For the first time in a long time, somebody wants Pessi. Catch wants Pessi. And win Pessi is exactly what Catch All-toys does.

Dana hands Pessi to Catch. She then gives the toy to her mother, who is already holding Chill in her other hand.

"AHHHHHHHH. AH. AH. AHHHHH!" Pessi hollers. Her eyes are still closed.

"Cut that out, you're fine! Stop screaming."

She hears a familiar voice. She opens her eyes. "AHHHHH!"

Chill covers Pessi's frown with his bendy straw. "Enough outta you!" He takes out the straw.

"AHHHHH!" Pessi screams once more. "I must be dead. I must be dreaming. This can't be real life."

"Well, it is, and we're together. So just relax, okay? Try to take a couple deep breaths," Chill tells her.

As Pessi tries to breathe, she can't help but think of her two pals still inside the game.

"I am elated for Pessi! What a day. Two of our friends are getting to go and experience the outside world! Aren't you excited, Sage! I'm so excited, I can just ROOOOOOAR!" Opti growls.

Sage smiles. "Yes, I am glad they are together. And there is more game left to play."

"atch Alltoys, you are now two for two! How do you feel?!" Dana taps elbows with Catch and places the microphone a foot away from her mouth.

"Umm, I feel good," Catch replies.

"Great! Well, you've now won Chill the Smoothie and Pessi the Sad Blobfish."

"I don't think she's sad," Catch interrupts. "I think somebody just put her smile on backwards."

Dana grins. The hearts around the room melt.

"You know what, I think you're right, Catch," Dana says. "I think you're absolutely right." She pauses, smiles, then continues. "Now, this is your final attempt, and if you win a toy here, you will be the first person to ever win the *What's Next Challenge*, and you will not only keep the next toy you catch, but you will also get your choice at a fourth toy! How does that sound?"

"Good," Catch says. It's clear she's laser focused.

"Alright, then, Catch Alltoys. For all the marbles, tell us one more time, Whaaaaat's Next?!"

"The *What's Next Challenge!*" Catch answers and then whispers to herself this time, "I don't know what's going to happen. If I win, I win. If I lose, I lose. But, no matter what, I learn, I learn."

And finally, cool as a cucumber, she looks over the crowd of people. She sees her parents, smiling and nodding. She looks at other kids biting their fingernails or covering their noses with their hands. And finally, she observes her new friend Ani, and she steps on the buttons so that the crane is over the back-right corner of the sea of prizes.

It seems as if the crane falls more gracefully this time, and it calmly grabs the robot from the abyss. It flawlessly transfers the doll over to the prize bin, as the crowd erupts with applause.

Catch Alltoys has won the *What's Next Challenge*.

Hooray for Sage! I may be all alone here now, but I mustn't panic. Nobody ever looks back on a situation and thinks, 'I really wish I would have panicked more!' Catch has a chance to choose any toy she wants now. I know she is going to pick me. I just know it." Opti sits up tall and flashes her fangs as best as she possibly can.

After the cheering subsides, Dana begins, "Catch All-toys, you are an amazing young woman! You have certainly lived up to your name. You have certainly lived up to Tomorrow World's expectation. And you have certainly won the *What's Next Challenge*! Now, it's your turn to actually walk inside *What's Next?!*'s four walls and choose the prize you want most. Nobody but me and the big boss upstairs has ever stepped foot inside *What's Next?!* But now, you will! Ladies and gentlemen, one more round of applause for Catch Alltoys!!!"

The crowd roars. As does Opti.

"Come with me!" Dana whispers to Catch. She unlocks

the hidden door in the glass, and Catch enters into the world of prizes. She knows exactly which one she wants. She swims through animals and stuffed mystical creatures, steps over game consoles, and moves a few boxes of candy to the side. And, finally, staring back at her with those sharp teeth and huge green eyes is Opti. Catch grips her with her right hand, tosses her up and catches her, and then she squeezes her tight.

Catch brings Opti over to the rest of her prizes—Pessi, Sage, and Chill—and she places them inside the bowl that sits atop the largest trophy she's ever seen. As the four *What's Next?!* toys are back together again, after what felt like an eternity of separation, they begin to chat.

"We did it! Catch is the most amazing and perfect owner! I am so happy to be back with you all. I just knew we were going to make it out as a group! I never lost faith for even a second! It was always supposed to be this way and no other way! What a day!" Opti says, hugging Pessi.

"I guess it is pretty cool," Chill offers with a half-smile. Even Pessi seems to be adjusting her mindset.

"I didn't think it was possible, but then again, here we are," she says, attempting to shrug.

Sage places his hands together. "I am glad we are all together in the moment. We may rejoice. But, even when the future seems 99.99 percent certain, and it seems certain that together is how we shall remain, there is always the other .01 percent. Something else can still happen unexpectedly, and we must be OK with that too. Although we are outside of *What's Next?!*, where anything can happen, we are still in Tomorrow World, where we never know what tomorrow will bring. We don't even know what one minute from now will bring. During times of uncertainty, we must lift up others. Please remember that."

"What else can happen?" Opti and Pessi say together.

And just as they finish their sentence, Dana announces that they have one more surprise in store for Catch. One more opportunity for their first ever *What's Next Challenge* winner.

The prize swap.

Catch walks a few steps behind Dana as she introduces her to Tomorrow World's wonderful wall of prizes. Usually, guests need a certain number of tickets to get these prizes. The more tickets, the bigger and better the prize. But today, Catch doesn't need tickets. She's won the *What's Next Challenge*. She can choose whatever she wants. But it will come at a cost. She'd have to give up one of the dolls she's already won.

As Catch slowly shifts her head from left to right, she sees everything she could have ever wanted. She sees every kid's dream right in front of her eyes. There are soccer balls, baseball mitts, and football helmets. There are more video games than she could ever play. There are bags and bags of candy, toy trucks, and even a brand new bicycle. As kids (and even some adults) shout out what they want her to pick (or really just what they want for themselves), Catch has a different idea.

She whispers something into Dana's ear. When Catch

finishes talking, Dana puts both hands over her heart and says, "Of course you can do that, sweetheart. Go right ahead."

And with Dana's permission, Catch goes over to her trophy bowl and holds Sage tightly. She gives him a hug.

Sage addresses his friends. "You may think you are losing me, but you are not. I will always be with you, so long as you never lose your faith. You always have your faith. Trust in that." He waves goodbye.

Catch breaks away from her hug with Sage and scans the crowd. After a few seconds of searching, she spots the person she's looking for. She walks over to Ani and extends her arm, offering up Sage.

"For your mom," Catch insists.

Ani accepts and gives Catch the colorful pen she received as a consolation prize. Catch flips the pen up into the air, and just as it's about to hit the ground, she bends quickly and snags it.

Pessi speaks, absolutely stunned. "What just happened? No, this can't be real. This can't be real—99.99 percent. Those are the facts. Those are the statistics. That is almost certain things will be the way they are supposed to be. How is that not so? What are we supposed to do without Sage? We're doomed! What do we do?"

"It's, uh, it's OK, Pessi. Let's, uh, let's look at the bright side of things. There's more space in the bowl?" Opti offers.

"I don't want more space in the bowl!" Pessi declares.

Opti tries again. "Umm, oh, I know. There are people out there who never got to meet Sage at all, but we did. Doesn't that help, Pessi? I know that must help!"

Pessi's frown widens. She tries to cover her eyes, but her fins are too tiny.

"How about this, Pessi. Sage is going with a really great girl! He is going to live a great life!"

"You don't know that!!!" Pessi fires back.

Chill has been sitting there thinking. The smoothie droplets have been running all down his straw and his cup. His friends can hear him sniffling. But for some reason, he doesn't care. He was slouched down in the trophy bowl, but now, he decides to fix his posture and speak. "I have something to say, you guys."

They both look at Chill.

"Everything OK, Chill?" Opti asks.

He sniffles one last time and breathes in and out through the opening of his straw. "I'm more than OK. Actually, *we're* more than OK. Think about it, you guys. Would the old robot want me to sit back and be indifferent in this situation? Would he want me to be chill and judgmental? Would

69

he want you to spread negative energy, Pessi, and cry and complain? Opti, would he want you to just think that we're going to agree with you because positivity is always supposed to trump negativity?" He looks at them both. They look back. He chuckles.

"You know what, guys? The steel-headed robot was right. Sage was my favorite toy in the entire world, and I didn't just listen to every word he said, but I truly *heard* every single word he said. I was just too afraid to give up my chill persona. I was too afraid to act different, to express that I really cared about something, someone. And you know what? Now he's gone, and I may never get the chance to share how I really felt about him. How important he was to me as a teacher and a guide and a voice about how we all should live our lives and handle the uncertainty of Tomorrow World. But, as Sage would say, now I must focus on what is within my control, and I know that I can control how I respond to this situation. I can pay tribute to Sage's memory by bringing us together and responding to this uncertain situation just as he would like us to. Without Sage here, these times are unprecedented. Nobody truly knows what to do. But I know what not to do. I know I can't be so chill, indifferent, self-absorbed, cold, and judgmental, because that serves as no help to the situation. I know you should not add more negativity to the pot, Pessi, and I know that you can't just think positivity is the only answer, right, Opti?"

"Right," they say, in unison.

Chill concludes, "So, what do you say, guys? Can we get through this with solidarity and unity and care for one another?" They huddle together and agree.

"By the way, Chill," Opti says. "I have faith that Sage knows how much he means to you."

"Yeah, me too," says Pessi.

"Faith." Chill laughs. "Now, I feel like we're all starting to get it."

The big boss upstairs is rarely seen on the arcade floor. But today is different. Today is magical. Today, something extraordinary happened in Tomorrow World, and the big boss knows it's the right time to make an appearance. The shadow from the tinted glass window disappears, and the big boss walks down the stairs. Dana, Catch, her parents, Ani, and the toys can hear the shoes click against each step, loudly and deliberately. It is dead silent. Everyone looks at the back of this mysterious figure, as she finally reaches level ground. She turns to face them all.

Mrs. Tamara Ward approaches the Alltoyses and Dana. She is ninety-one years old with powdery white hair and unwrinkled skin. She wears bright red lipstick. She is not quite five feet tall, but her presence can be heard and felt from hundreds of miles away.

"Weren't expecting little old me, now, were you? I guess that's the beauty of sitting upstairs in my office most of the day. Oftentimes, when people just hear 'the big boss,' and they are uncertain as to who that is, I am the last thing they expect! Sometimes, I just come down here and walk around, and nobody knows I built this place from the ground up almost fifty years ago! Uncertainty has its positives and negatives, but the key is not to judge it. Just embrace it and accept it, no?"

The Alltoyses laugh. Dana smiles.

"That is some special little girl you have there." Mrs. Ward points at Catch. "Say, Dana. What did she whisper to you before giving away her prize?"

"Well, I'll let her tell you. Catch, can you come here for a second, please?"

Catch trots over with Ani.

"Hi, Catch. That was some show you put on today. I'm Mrs. Ward, owner of Tomorrow World, and I would like to personally thank you for being here and for winning the *What's Next Challenge*! You have given a lot of kids hope and something to look forward to, you know. Elbow tap!" Catch elbow-taps Mrs. Ward. "We were curious, though, Catch. What did you whisper to Dana before you swapped toys with your new friend?"

"I asked Dana if, even though I was supposed to exchange with a toy from the wall—because nobody had ever done this before and won the challenge—could I do something different. I told her that I made a new friend named Ani who tries all the time to win a prize but never has. And Ani said that if she were to win, she'd want the robot in the back to give to her mom, because she's an inventor, so I made sure on my last try to catch that doll, so I could give it to her for her mom. So, I asked Dana if I could swap with somebody with a consolation prize instead of from the wonderful wall of prizes. I have enough dolls and toys. I was glad Ani just had the pen."

"Bless your beautiful little heart." Mrs. Ward blushes. "You are absolutely correct, Catch. When there is no right answer, it is important to try new things, do the best that you can for yourself, but ultimately try your hardest to do right by others. It is a time when we can be innovative and creative, generous and altruistic, and you have really shown us this." And with that, Mrs. Ward tosses Catch a key she'd been holding in her left hand. "A key to Tomorrow World. You are always welcome here, Catch. Always."

Mrs. Ward and Dana inform the Alltoyses, Ani, and Ani's dad that unfortunately it's time for Tomorrow World to close down for the day. The three toys in the bowl overhear this conversation, and Pessi begins to panic.

"This is it! This is where it really happens! We are about to leave Tomorrow World officially and enter into. Enter into. Enter into." It seems Pessi may be malfunctioning.

"Enter into what?" Opti interjects.

"The PARKING LOT. I don't want to go to the parking lot. That's where I've seen the people in the winter jackets with the boots, and the weather is not nice, and there may be snow. It's not for me. I'm just going to stay here, you guys. Go on without me."

Chill can feel his liquid boiling up, but he decides to cool down. He considers what Sage would say. Probably something about how nobody has ever looked back and said, "Oh, I wish I would have yelled at her more, or judged her more, or urged her to panic more." He takes a big slurp and he speaks.

"Faith will guide us through this. Solidarity, cooperation, and not focusing on the negative will be our core principles. We will be alert as to what is out there, but we will remain calm. Hey, Pess, remember last week when that kid choked on his hot dog?"

"Sure do, he almost died!" Pessi replies.

"Well, thankfully, he was fine, and kids were laughing, but it was no laughing matter. Luckily there was a nurse in the building. An amazing, miraculous first responder, and do you remember the first thing she said as she approached the situation?"

"No, what was it?" Pessi asks.

"She told everyone to remain calm, and then she began to delegate. 'Somebody call 911, somebody grab some water, somebody find his parents.' She asked onlookers the right questions, she gathered information, and then she performed the Heimlich, not knowing if it was going to work, but giving some sort of solution a try. And it didn't work at first, but she learned from the first attempt, tried it again, and what happened, Pess?"

"The kid coughed up a quarter of a hot dog?"

"That's right. He coughed up that quarter dog, and everybody was OK in the end. That's what happens when we all support one another. We are going to be OK in the end. I promise."

Pessi bobs her head, but sadly, she's still frowning.

Catch asks her parents if she can hold her new friends as they walk to the car. They agree, and Catch hugs Opti with her right arm, and she attempts to hold Pessi and Chill in her left.

But as soon as Pessi leaves the bowl, a feeling of uneasiness overtakes her body and she stretches her little fins as far as possible, attempting to escape Catch's grip.

"I don't want to leave Tomorrow World! I don't want to find out what's next! I just want to stay here!" Pessi hollers.

And with that, Pessi jumps out of Catch's arm, and begins to fall to the ground. Catch goes to grab her with two fingers, and latches onto her little fin, but there is too much tension. Pessi's fin rips off, and in the process, Catch also drops Chill and Opti on the floor.

In that instant, Catch Alltoys experienced her first ever drop.

Tears begin to stream down her face. She can't believe she dropped her new friends and one of her friends has already ripped.

Chill is ready to explode, but again, he pauses. He waits.

"Oof!" Opti yelps. "I'm OK, all good!"

Pessi stares straight ahead. "She tried to catch me. She

tried to catch me, but I ripped away. And I made her cry. Oh no, what did I do? I made our new friend cry, and I made her drop me, and I made her drop you guys, too, and now here we are on the floor, and we could have been hurt! I can't believe how much worse my negativity made everything. I can't believe my desire to escape the uncertainty made things so terrible for everyone else! I am so sorry. I don't deserve to be taken out of Tomorrow World."

Chill responds. "You see, Pessi, there is not just one proper response to uncertainty. As the name suggests, it is something nobody can ever be certain about. But there is one response that does lead to worse outcomes, which you just witnessed. When you panic, when you spread pessimism, when you complain and when you try to escape uncertainty and run away, it causes a negative ripple effect. It impacts other people. That is why Opti and I fell too. That is why your fin ripped off. That is why Catch is crying. This ripple effect can be extremely dangerous for the people we love most, and as the old robot told me, we never want to do anything that can hurt these people. Don't you agree?"

Pessi still stares straight ahead, trance-like. "Catch loves me. She chose me out of all the other toys. She tried to catch me. I let her down. From this point forward, I pledge to embrace uncertainty and try my best to not think about winning or losing, but rather just learning and growing through each situation. Just like Catch says: *I don't know what's going to happen. If I win, I win. If I lose, I lose. But, no matter what, I learn, I learn.*"

"Uncertainty is what you make of it," Chill agrees.

"Aw, sweetie, don't cry. You just tripped. Don't worry about it. It happens." Mrs. Ward consoles Catch. She takes some glue out of her pocket and dabs it against Pessi's missing fin. She reattaches it with ease. "Here you go, my love."

Catch wipes the tears away, and she thanks Mrs. Ward for fixing her toy and for an amazing day. Again, she squeezes Opti tight in her right arm, and she holds Pessi and Chill in her left.

The Alltoyses, Mrs. Ward, Dana, Ani, and Ani's dad walk toward the exit of Tomorrow World. They walk past the smells of the cafeteria, the sounds of the machines, and the main attraction of the day—*What's Next?!* Where anything can happen! But as they walk by, Pessi notices something else written on the game. She could never see it because she was always trapped in her bottom corner, and to the toys inside it looked illegible. But in teeny, tiny writing on the left-hand corner just beside where contestants insert coins to play, there is a phrase so small that oftentimes people miss it.

The phrase reads: "You always get a prize." Pessi thinks about that. She finally realizes what the gibberish they had always stared at from inside the game actually meant. No matter the uncertainty that lies ahead, there will always be a prize. You can learn and grow from any situation.

Mrs. Ward and Dana wave goodbye as the doors slide open. Ani, her father, the Alltoyses, and Catch's new friends leave Tomorrow World, and enter the parking lot.

Pessi doesn't even make a peep.

"We really ought to make that sign about consolation prizes bigger, boss," Dana insists. "So many kids forgot to get their prizes after striking out at *What's Next?!* today."

Mrs. Ward smiles. "That's a great idea, Dana, let's do it. It's important everybody knows that there is still a prize no matter what happens." They wave goodbye one last time, and they lock the doors behind them.

As the families arrive at their cars, the adults urge Ani and Catch to say their goodbyes. "Elbow tap!" Catch insists. Ani obliges. They say goodbye for now, and they get into their cars.

While the Alltoyses drive down the highway to their hotel, Catch asks her parents if she and Ani can have a play-date sometime soon. They happily let her know they think they can make that happen. As Catch sits in the back seat and plays with each of her new friends, she notices a car passing by. She presses her head up against the window and screams, "Look, Mom and Dad! It's Ani!"

And as Catch and her parents wave at Ani and her dad, the dolls in the back seat wave at something else.

His journey began on the top right-hand side of the plethora of toys, and although he often seems to move around throughout the day, something almost always brings him back to the top right corner. Something about it just feels right.

In the top right corner of the window in Ani's car, Sage is waving back at Chill, Pessi, and Opti.

Opti roars with enthusiasm.

Chill blows bubbles with joy.

And with the magic that is Tomorrow World, and for the first time ever, Pessi's frown turns into a smile.

THIS BOOK IS POWERED BY "IMAGITIVETATION"

Imagitivetation is a combination of imagination, interpretation, creativity, and implementation.

The author used his *imagitivetation* to craft this story for you. He imagined what a world would look like in which uncertainty was everywhere, but there were key responses that made the feeling a bit easier to handle. He interpreted why this was the world he wanted to build. He creatively designed each character, each response, based off of his own life experiences and people he knew. Finally, he implemented his plan by putting words on paper.

Jordan urges you to use your *imagitivetation* as you read this book and all of his other works. Imagine your ideal world. Interpret why this is the world you want to live in. Get creative and make a plan for how to get there. Begin to implement that plan.

It will make your personal growth journey that much more fun and exciting.

For more about imagitivetation, and to read more stories like this, check out Jordan's website, Jordan-Gross.com. This is a community of storytellers, dreamers, lil' books, and authors trailblazing through the land of personal development via creative storytelling.

GENERAL DISCUSSION QUESTIONS

1. Which character do you resonate with the most? Why?
2. Do you think there are right and wrong answers in uncertain situations?
3. How can you navigate uncertain situations with somebody who thinks very differently from you?
4. How do you think you should change your response to uncertainty after reading this?
5. Are there other ways to manage uncertainty that were not mentioned in the book?
6. Who would you become if everything changed?

REFLECTION QUESTIONS FOR *PESSI* PEOPLE

1. How do your actions impact those around you?
2. Why do you think this way during uncertain situations? Do you think this is the right way?
3. Which character do you want to be more like the next time you face uncertainty?

REFLECTION QUESTIONS FOR *OPTI* PEOPLE

1. What are the downsides of your approach to uncertainty?
2. Do you think positivity is always the answer? When may it not be?
3. How can you change your behavior so as not to upset those around you who may think differently?

REFLECTION QUESTIONS FOR *CHILL* PEOPLE

1. What are the upsides to this way of thinking? Downsides?
2. What minor adjustments can you make to your behavior to better suit uncertain situations?
3. How can you teach others to be a bit more like you?

REFLECTION QUESTIONS FOR *SAGE* PEOPLE

1. Why do you think others have trouble accepting a lack of control?
2. What can you do when people disagree with your way of thinking?
3. Is it difficult to constantly maintain this way of thinking? How do you do it?

IMAGITIVETATING YOUR DREAM LIFE EXERCISE

Remember Mad Libs? Well, here is your chance to unleash your inner child and play it again! Except this time, instead of creating a fun party game, you'll be creating the life of your dreams by using your imagitivetation.

My name is _____, and I
your name

believe that I can use my imagitivetation to live the life of my dreams. Let's get started.

IMAGINATION: WHAT IF?

I am in the final years of my life, and I am _____.
# of years old

I am sitting in my _____ talking to
type of seat

_____ reflecting on what a
somebody very important in your life

beautiful life it has been. I am so proud that I have been

able to _____,

_____,

and _____,
list three accomplishments you wish to achieve in your personal life

and I am so grateful that I have been able to _____

_____

_____,

_____

_____,

and _____

_____.
list three accomplishments you wish to achieve in your professional life

It was a difficult choice not to pursue _____

_____

_____,
something in your life that feels safe, normal, but does not excite you

but ultimately deciding to_____
_____
_____

*something you feel like you should be doing, even though it is
scary and maybe unorthodox*

gave me a sense of meaning and fulfillment every day of
my life that I wouldn't trade for anything. I looked at the
lives of people like _____,

_____, and _____,

name three role models, specific people, or types of people

and I realized that I wanted to be like them because of

their _____, _____,

and _____,

list three desirable characteristics

as opposed to _____,

_____, and _____

*name three types of people or specific individuals whose lives you do not wish
to emulate*

because of their _____,

_____, and _____.

list three undesirable characteristics

It is because of these decisions that I have truly lived the
life of my dreams.

INTERPRETATION: WHY?

1. Why did I choose to be that age? Why was that the person I chose to speak to?
2. Why were these three personal accomplishments important to me?
3. Why were these three professional accomplishments important to me?
4. Why were these the people I wanted to be like?
5. Why were these the people I no longer wanted to be like?
6. Why do I want to make any change at all? Why do I not want to keep going down the same path?

CREATIVITY: HOW?

I am _____, and I have just decided to live the life of
your current age

my dreams. I have already imagined myself years in the future, and I have interpreted why this is the life I want to live. Now, I am sitting in my _____,
wherever you currently are

and I must creatively design how I can actively begin

pursuing my dream life. I will read _____,
_____, _____
_____, and _____.
five books related to your chosen path

I will listen to _____, _____,
_____, _____,
and _____.
five talks or podcasts related to your chosen path

I will talk to _____, _____,
_____, _____,
and _____.
five people who can advise you on your path

I will start with the end in mind, and then reverse engineer
my process by choosing _____,
_____, and _____
three key milestones

that I must reach on my way to where I ultimately want to
be. I will enjoy every moment of this journey to living the
life of my dreams.

IMPLEMENTATION: WHAT?

1. What does success mean for you on this new journey?
2. What will you do when you feel like giving up?
3. What will you try that you have never tried before?

ACKNOWLEDGMENTS

My deepest thanks go out to all of the first-line responders around the world. Thank you for being heroes. Thank you for risking your lives in the outside world every day, so I could be safe inside my home and have the ability to write this.

There are a lot of people who help bring an author's idea from dream to reality, but nobody is more important than you, the reader. Thank you for taking the time to venture through the doors of Tomorrow World and learn a little bit more about my friends Opti, Pessi, Sage, Chill, and Catch. Your support and belief matter to me most, and I am forever grateful.

People are the most important part of my life, and I interact with so many on a daily basis. While I cannot include everyone here, please know that I am thankful for you all. I plan to write many more books, so if you ever really want a personal shout-out, message me, and I'll include you in the next one!

Mom, Dad, and Adam: Who would have thought that any of my silly ideas would ever come to life? Thanks for always listening with a smile.

This book is for Grandma Harriet and Grandma Elly, the real-life Opti and Pessi. Keep being exactly who you are. It's worked for the past ninety-plus years.

In loving memory of Grandpa Morty and Grandpa David. Chill and Sage. Extremely different people, but both with hearts the size of the question marks in front of the Tomorrow World doors.

There is no greater gift than someone's belief in you. Thank you, Rich Keller, for supporting me and encouraging me to change the world.

A very special thank-you to Jon Gordon, not just for providing the foreword, but also for putting your name on the line and introducing me to your first ever publisher and now mine, Matt Holt. Thank you for believing in me enough to make a connection.

And finally, thank you to Matt Holt and the rest of the team at BenBella Books, Matt Holt Books. Matt, I am truly in awe of your willingness to take a chance on me. I still don't think you know how much it means to me. Thank you, Robb Pearlman and Michael Fedison for a smooth and seamless editing process; Sarah Avinger for the creative cover; Jennifer Canzoneri for your awesome marketing strategy; as well as Glenn Yeffeth, Adrienne Lang, Monica Lowry, Leah Wilson, Aida Herrera, Alicia Kania, and Katie Hollister for the phenomenal work you do, and Ralph Voltz for his wonderful illustrations.

ABOUT THE AUTHOR

Jordan is reimagining personal development. He believes that personal development is a never-ending process of imagining who you want to be, interpreting why you want to be that person, creating a plan to get there, and then implementing that plan in the most enjoyable and fulfilling way possible. Through his platform *imagitivetation* (imagination + interpretation + creativity + implementation), he helps guide people to think differently and make daring changes in their lives. Jordan is trailblazing in the personal development field by using creative storytelling to allow people to gather their own insights from the characters he creates and the stories he shares.

Jordan is a Northwestern and Kellogg School of Management graduate where he studied absolutely nothing to do with writing. He's a former startup founder, restaurant manager, and soccer goalie. A solopreneur, podcast host, a

2x TEDx speaker, an editor, and coach, he is also the #1 bestselling author of *Getting COMFY: Your Morning Guide to Daily Happiness* and *The Journey to Cloud Nine.*

Jordan loves people and would be overjoyed to chat with you. Connect with him on Linkedin (linkedin.com/in/jordangross9/) and stay up to date with his creative stories on Medium (medium.com/@jordan.c.gross2016).